VERONICA RUFF

THE EASTER DEVOTIONAL

40 Days of Prayer, Reflection and Family Devotions for Lent and Easter

First published by Integrity Press 2026

Copyright © 2026 by Veronica Ruff

Veronica Ruff asserts the moral right to be identified as the author of this work.

No part of this publication may be reproduced, stored in a retrieval system, or transmitted in any form or by any means—electronic, mechanical, photocopying, recording, or otherwise—without the prior written permission of the author, except for brief quotations used in reviews or scholarly articles.

Scripture quotations taken from the Holy Bible, New International Version®, NIV®. Copyright © 1973, 1978, 1984, 2011 by Biblica, Inc.™ Used by permission. All rights reserved worldwide.

This devotional is intended for personal and family use. It is not a substitute for pastoral care, professional counseling, or theological instruction. The reflections, prayers, and activities are offered as encouragement and inspiration, and should be adapted to the unique needs of each household. Readers are encouraged to seek guidance from trusted pastors, mentors, or counsellors for deeper study or personal concerns.

The publisher and author disclaim any liability for misuse of the material or for outcomes resulting from its application beyond its intended devotional purpose.

Cover design and interior layout by Veronica Ruff. Illustrations by Veronica Ruff. Published in NSW, Australia.

Printed and distributed via Amazon KDP and IngramSpark.

First edition

ISBN: 978-1-7644953-0-1

This book was professionally typeset on Reedsy.
Find out more at reedsy.com

Dedication

To every family seeking quiet connection, to every child who asks deep questions, to every parent who prays in whispers—may these pages become a place of renewal, a rhythm of grace, a sanctuary of love.

And to the One who makes all things new—this offering is Yours.

Contents

Foreword	ii
Preface	iii
Introduction	1
How to Use This Book	2
What is Lent?	3
Week 1: Grace	4
Week 2: Renewal	11
Week 3: Peace	18
Week 4: Joy	24
Week 5: Safety	30
Week 6: Holy Week — The Triduum	36
Family Notes & Journaling	48
About the Author	53

Foreword

Lent and Easter invite us into a sacred rhythm of reflection, prayer, and renewal. These forty days are not only a journey toward the cross and resurrection, but also an opportunity to pause, breathe, and draw closer to God in the midst of daily life.

This devotional was created with families in mind. Each day offers a simple prayer, a reflection prompt, a Scripture reading, and a family activity designed to nurture connection and faith. Whether gathered around the table, sharing a quiet moment before bed, or walking together outdoors, these devotions are meant to be woven gently into your life.

The heart of this book is sanctuary: a place where words, prayers, and rituals can bring comfort, clarity, and joy. My hope is that these pages will help you notice God's presence in small moments, strengthen your bonds as a family, and remind you that renewal and resurrection are always possible.

May this devotional be a companion on your path through Lent and Easter, guiding you with peace, safety, and joy.

Preface

The Easter Devotional

40 Days of Prayer, Reflection and Family Devotions for Lent and Easter

Introduction

Step into the story of Easter with your family.

This devotional offers forty days of Scripture, reflection and prayer designed to nurture faith and connection across generations. Each week closes with a family journaling prompt, inviting you to pause, share, and record memories together.

With gentle rhythms, creative space for notes, and themes of gratitude, forgiveness, renewal, joy, and resurrection, this book becomes more than a devotional—it becomes a keepsake of your family's journey through Lent and Easter.

Whether gathered around the table, in quiet prayer, or during bedtime reflection, these pages invite you to experience Easter not only as a season of faith, but as a sanctuary of love, hope, and renewal.

How to Use This Book

This devotional is designed to be simple, flexible, and family-friendly. Each day includes five elements:

Daily Prayer — a short prayer to begin or end your day.

Reflection Prompt — a question to help you pause and think about your faith journey.

Scripture Reading — a verse from the Bible to anchor the devotion.

Family Devotion Activity — a practical way to share faith together at home.

Closing Blessing — a gentle word of encouragement to carry with you.

What is Lent?

Lent is a season in the Christian calendar that prepares us for Easter. It begins on **Ash Wednesday** and lasts for **forty days**, not counting Sundays. These forty days recall the time Jesus spent fasting and praying in the wilderness before beginning His ministry.

Week 1: Grace

WEEK 1: GRACE

Theme: Forgiveness, kindness, and second chances

Day 1: The Gift of Grace

Daily Prayer: Lord, thank You for loving me before I even knew You. Help me receive Your grace with open hands.

Reflection Prompt: What does grace feel like when you've made a mistake?

Scripture Reading: Ephesians 2:8–9 — *For it is by grace you have been saved...*

Family Devotion Activity: Light a candle and name one thing you're grateful for that you didn't earn.

Closing Blessing: May grace wrap around you like morning light—gentle, undeserved, and always enough.

Day 2: Forgiveness Begins Here

Daily Prayer: Jesus, teach me to forgive as You forgive—freely, fully, and without keeping score.

Reflection Prompt: Is there someone you need to forgive or ask forgiveness from?

Scripture Reading: Luke 6:37 — *Forgive, and you will be forgiven.*

Family Devotion Activity: Write a short note of apology or forgiveness to someone, even if you don't send it.

Closing Blessing: May your heart be lightened by forgiveness, and your home softened by mercy.

Day 3: Kindness in Action

Daily Prayer: God of compassion, help me choose kindness even when it's hard.

Reflection Prompt: When did someone's kindness change your day or your life?

Scripture Reading: Colossians 3:12 — *Clothe yourselves with compassion, kindness...*

Family Devotion Activity: Do one secret act of kindness for someone in your family today.

Closing Blessing: May kindness ripple through your home like sunlight on water—gentle, bright, and healing.

Day 4: Second Chances

Daily Prayer: Lord, thank You for never giving up on me. Help me offer second chances to others.

Reflection Prompt: What does a second chance look like in your life right now?

Scripture Reading: Lamentations 3:22–23 — *His mercies are new every morning.*

Family Devotion Activity: Share a story of a time you were given a second chance.

Closing Blessing: May today be a fresh start, full of mercy, hope, and grace.

Day 5: Grace in the Everyday

Daily Prayer: Jesus, help me see Your grace in ordinary moments—in laughter, in quiet, in mess.

Reflection Prompt: Where did you notice grace today?

Scripture Reading: Romans 5:1–2 — *We have peace with God… through whom we have gained access by faith into this grace…*

Family Devotion Activity: Take a walk and name five things that feel like grace.

Closing Blessing: May grace surprise you in the smallest places and remind you—you are deeply loved.

Day 6: Grace for Others

Daily Prayer: Lord, help me extend grace to others, especially when I feel impatient or hurt.

Reflection Prompt: Who in your life needs grace today?

Scripture Reading: Matthew 5:7 — *Blessed are the merciful…*

Family Devotion Activity: Create a "grace jar"—fill it with kind notes or prayers for others.

Closing Blessing: May your words be soft with grace, and your heart open to mercy.

Day 7: Living Gracefully

Daily Prayer: God, let my life reflect Your grace—not just in words, but in how I live.

Reflection Prompt: What does it mean to live gracefully?

Scripture Reading: Titus 2:11–12 — *The grace of God... teaches us to say 'No' to ungodliness...*

Family Devotion Activity: Draw or write what "grace" looks like to you. Share it with your family.

Closing Blessing: May grace guide your steps, soften your speech, and shape your story.

Family Journaling Prompt

What did grace look like in our home this week?

Journal Notes:

_____
_____
_____
_____
_____
_____
_____
_____
_____
_____
_____
_____
_____
_____
_____

THE EASTER DEVOTIONAL

_____
_____
_____
_____

Week 2: Renewal

Theme: Spring, healing, and new beginnings

Day 8: New Every Morning

Daily Prayer: Lord, thank You for the gift of new beginnings. Help me wake with hope and trust.

Reflection Prompt: What would you like to leave behind—and what would you like to begin again?

Scripture Reading: Psalm 143:8 — *Let the morning bring me word of Your unfailing love...*

Family Devotion Activity: Step outside at sunrise or early morning. Breathe deeply and name one hope for today.

Closing Blessing: May this morning bring you peace, and may renewal rise with the light.

Day 9: Healing in His Hands

Daily Prayer: Jesus, I place my wounds—seen and unseen—in Your healing hands.

Reflection Prompt: Where do you need healing today—in body, heart, or relationships?

Scripture Reading: Psalm 147:3 — *He heals the brokenhearted...*

Family Devotion Activity: Draw or write a prayer for healing and place it under a candle or cross.

Closing Blessing: May healing flow gently through your home, restoring what was broken with grace.

Day 10: Spring Within

Daily Prayer: Creator God, let Your renewal bloom in me like spring after winter.

Reflection Prompt: What signs of growth do you see in yourself or your family?

Scripture Reading: Isaiah 43:19 — *See, I am doing a new thing…*

Family Devotion Activity: Plant a seed or bulb together. Talk about what it needs to grow.

Closing Blessing: May your spirit bloom with courage, and your home be a garden of grace.

Day 11: Letting Go

Daily Prayer: God, help me release what no longer serves me. Make space for Your renewal.

Reflection Prompt: What are you holding onto that you might gently let go?

Scripture Reading: Ecclesiastes 3:6 — *A time to keep and a time to throw away.*

Family Devotion Activity: Choose one item to donate or release. Bless it as you let it go.

Closing Blessing: May release bring relief, and may empty hands be ready to receive.

Day 12: Restoring Joy

Daily Prayer: Lord, restore to me the joy of Your presence. Let laughter return.

Reflection Prompt: When did you last feel truly joyful?

Scripture Reading: Psalm 51:12 — *Restore to me the joy of Your salvation...*

Family Devotion Activity: Share a funny story or memory together. Let laughter be your prayer.

Closing Blessing: May joy rise again like spring rain—unexpected, refreshing, and full of life.

Day 13: Growing Together

Daily Prayer: Jesus, help us grow together in love, patience, and understanding.

Reflection Prompt: How have you grown as a family this past year?

Scripture Reading: Ephesians 4:15 — *We will grow to become... the mature body of Christ.*

Family Devotion Activity: Create a "growth tree"—draw a tree and write ways you've grown on each branch.

Closing Blessing: May your roots deepen in love, and your branches stretch toward light.

Day 14: The Promise of Renewal

Daily Prayer: God of resurrection, remind me that renewal is always possible—even when I feel weary.

Reflection Prompt: What promise of God do you need to hold onto today?

Scripture Reading: Revelation 21:5 — *I am making everything new!*

Family Devotion Activity: Write a family promise to support each other in renewal. Hang it somewhere visible.

Closing Blessing: May renewal be your rhythm, and may hope be your heartbeat.

Family Journaling Prompt

Where did we notice renewal in our lives this week? How did God surprise us with new beginnings?

Journal Notes:

_____
_____
_____
_____
_____
_____
_____
_____
_____
_____
_____
_____
_____
_____
_____
_____
_____

WEEK 2: RENEWAL

Week 3: Peace

WEEK 3: PEACE

Theme: Reconciliation, stillness, and sanctuary

Day 15: The Gift of Peace

Daily Prayer: Lord, let Your peace settle in my heart like calm waters.

Reflection Prompt: Where do you most need peace right now?

Scripture Reading: John 14:27 — *Peace I leave with you; my peace I give you...*

Family Devotion Activity: Sit together in silence for one minute. Notice how peace feels.

Closing Blessing: May peace guard your heart and mind, steady and sure.

Day 16: Reconciliation

Daily Prayer: Jesus, help me mend broken relationships with humility and love.

Reflection Prompt: Is there someone you could reach out to in reconciliation?

Scripture Reading: Matthew 5:9 — *Blessed are the peacemakers...*

Family Devotion Activity: Write a prayer for someone you'd like to reconcile with.

Closing Blessing: May peace restore what was lost and heal what was wounded.

Day 17: Still Waters

Daily Prayer: Shepherd God, lead me beside still waters and restore my soul.

Reflection Prompt: What helps you feel calm and restored?

Scripture Reading: Psalm 23:2–3 — *He leads me beside quiet waters...*

Family Devotion Activity: Listen to gentle music together and breathe deeply.

Closing Blessing: May stillness refresh you and peace renew your spirit.

Day 18: Peace in the Storm

Daily Prayer: Lord, calm the storms within me and around me.

Reflection Prompt: What storms—big or small—are you facing today?

Scripture Reading: Mark 4:39 — *He rebuked the wind and said... 'Quiet! Be still!*

Family Devotion Activity: Draw a storm turning into sunshine. Talk about God's calming presence.

Closing Blessing: May peace steady you when winds rise and storms roar.

Day 19: Sanctuary at Home

Daily Prayer: God, make my home a sanctuary of peace and welcome.

Reflection Prompt: What makes your home feel peaceful?

Scripture Reading: Isaiah 32:18 — *My people will live in peaceful dwelling places...*

Family Devotion Activity: Create a "peace corner" with a candle, cross, or flower.

Closing Blessing: May peace dwell in your home and flow through every room.

Day 20: Peace with Creation

Daily Prayer: Creator God, help me live in harmony with Your creation.

Reflection Prompt: How can you care for the earth as an act of peace?

Scripture Reading: Romans 8:19–21 — *Creation waits in eager expectation...*

Family Devotion Activity: Spend time outdoors noticing signs of peace in nature.

Closing Blessing: May peace root you in creation's rhythm and renew your spirit.

Day 21: The Prince of Peace

Daily Prayer: Jesus, Prince of Peace, reign in my heart and in the world.

Reflection Prompt: How does Christ's peace differ from the world's peace?

Scripture Reading: Isaiah 9:6 — *He will be called... Prince of Peace.*

Family Devotion Activity: Light a candle and pray for peace in the world.

Closing Blessing: May Christ's peace guide your steps and shine through your life.

Family Journaling Prompt

Where did we experience peace this week—in our hearts, our home, or our relationships?

Journal Notes:

Week 4: Joy

WEEK 4: JOY

Theme: Celebrations of hope, laughter, and resurrection

Day 22: Joy Comes in the Morning

Daily Prayer: Lord, thank You that joy rises like the sun after a long night.

Reflection Prompt: When have you felt joy after a season of sorrow?

Scripture Reading: Psalm 30:5 — *Weeping may stay for the night, but rejoicing comes in the morning.*

Family Devotion Activity: Watch the sunrise together and name one joy you're grateful for.

Closing Blessing: May joy greet you with the dawn and carry you through the day.

Day 23: Strength in Joy

Daily Prayer: God, remind me that Your joy is my strength.

Reflection Prompt: How does joy give you strength in hard times?

Scripture Reading: Nehemiah 8:10 — *The joy of the Lord is your strength.*

Family Devotion Activity: Share one thing that makes each family member feel strong.

Closing Blessing: May joy empower you to face challenges with courage and hope.

Day 24: Joy in Creation

Daily Prayer: Creator God, let me delight in the beauty of Your world.

Reflection Prompt: What part of creation brings you joy today?

Scripture Reading: Psalm 19:1 — *The heavens declare the glory of God...*

Family Devotion Activity: Take a walk outdoors and point out joyful signs of creation.

Closing Blessing: May joy bloom in your spirit like flowers in spring.

Day 25: Joy in Community

Daily Prayer: Lord, thank You for the joy of family, friends, and fellowship.

Reflection Prompt: Who brings joy into your life?

Scripture Reading: Philippians 1:3–4 — *I always pray with joy because of your partnership...*

Family Devotion Activity: Call or message someone to share a joyful memory.

Closing Blessing: May joy deepen your connections and brighten your relationships.

Day 26: Joy in Worship

Daily Prayer: God, let my worship be filled with joy and gratitude.

Reflection Prompt: How does worship bring you joy?

Scripture Reading: Psalm 100:1–2 — *Shout for joy to the Lord... worship the Lord with gladness.*

Family Devotion Activity: Sing a hymn or worship song together.

Closing Blessing: May joy lift your voice and fill your heart with praise.

Day 27: Joy in Small Things

Daily Prayer: Lord, help me notice joy in everyday moments.

Reflection Prompt: What small thing brought you joy today?

Scripture Reading: Matthew 6:28 — *See how the flowers of the field grow...*

Family Devotion Activity: Share three small joys from your day.

Closing Blessing: May joy surprise you in the ordinary and remind you of God's care.

Day 28: Joy of Resurrection

Daily Prayer: Jesus, thank You for the joy of resurrection and eternal life.

Reflection Prompt: How does the resurrection fill you with joy?

Scripture Reading: 1 Peter 1:3 — *He has given us new birth into a living hope...*

Family Devotion Activity: Decorate eggs or flowers as symbols of new life.

Closing Blessing: May resurrection joy renew your spirit and brighten your home.

Family Journaling Prompt

Where did joy surprise us this week—in laughter, in worship, or in small everyday moments?

Journal Notes:

_____
_____
_____
_____
_____
_____
_____
_____
_____
_____
_____
_____
_____
_____
_____
_____
_____
_____
_____
_____

Week 5: Safety

WEEK 5: SAFETY

Theme: Protection, guidance, and family bonds

Day 29: God Our Refuge

Daily Prayer: Lord, be my refuge and fortress. Keep me safe in Your care.

Reflection Prompt: Where do you turn when you feel unsafe or uncertain?

Scripture Reading: Psalm 46:1 — *God is our refuge and strength, an ever-present help in trouble.*

Family Devotion Activity: Build a "refuge space" at home—a quiet corner with a candle or cross.

Closing Blessing: May God's refuge surround you with peace and protection.

Day 30: Guardian of Our Steps

Daily Prayer: Jesus, guide my steps and keep me from stumbling.

Reflection Prompt: When have you felt God guiding your path?

Scripture Reading: Psalm 121:3 — *He will not let your foot slip...*

Family Devotion Activity: Take a short walk together, praying for God's guidance with each step.

Closing Blessing: May your journey be steady, and your steps secure in His care.

Day 31: Shelter Under His Wings

Daily Prayer: Lord, hide me under the shadow of Your wings.

Reflection Prompt: What does it mean to feel sheltered by God?

Scripture Reading: Psalm 91:4 — *He will cover you with His feathers...*

Family Devotion Activity: Draw a picture of wings and write prayers for safety inside them.

Closing Blessing: May His wings shelter you, and His love shield you always.

Day 32: Safe in Community

Daily Prayer: God, thank You for the safety of family and community.

Reflection Prompt: Who makes you feel safe and supported?

Scripture Reading: Ecclesiastes 4:9–10 — *Two are better than one... if either falls, one can help the other up.*

Family Devotion Activity: Share one way each person helps the family feel safe.

Closing Blessing: May your bonds of love be strong, and your home a sanctuary of safety.

Day 33: Protection in Prayer

Daily Prayer: Lord, place Your protection around me like a shield.

Reflection Prompt: How does prayer make you feel safe?

Scripture Reading: Proverbs 18:10 — *The name of the Lord is a fortified tower...*

Family Devotion Activity: Pray together for protection over your home and loved ones.

Closing Blessing: May prayer be your shield, and God's name your strong tower.

Day 34: Safety in Trust

Daily Prayer: Jesus, help me trust You fully, even when I feel afraid.

Reflection Prompt: What fears can you place in God's hands today?

Scripture Reading: Isaiah 26:3 — *You will keep in perfect peace those whose minds are steadfast...*

Family Devotion Activity: Write down a fear and place it in a "trust box."

Closing Blessing: May trust quiet your fears and bring you peace.

Day 35: Eternal Safety

Daily Prayer: Lord, thank You that my life is safe in Your eternal love.

Reflection Prompt: How does God's promise of eternal life bring you comfort?

Scripture Reading: John 10:28 — *No one will snatch them out of my hand.*

Family Devotion Activity: Light a candle and reflect on God's eternal promise of safety.

Closing Blessing: May eternal safety in Christ give you courage and hope.

Family Journaling Prompt

WEEK 5: SAFETY

Where did we feel God's safety this week—in our home, our prayers, or our trust?

Journal Notes:

_____
_____
_____
_____
_____
_____
_____
_____
_____
_____
_____
_____
_____
_____
_____
_____
_____
_____
_____
_____
_____

Week 6: Holy Week — The Triduum

WEEK 6: HOLY WEEK — THE TRIDUUM

Palm Sunday: Welcoming the King

Daily Prayer: Lord Jesus, we welcome You with joy. Teach us to honour You not just with words, but with our lives.

Reflection Prompt: How can you welcome Jesus into your home and heart today?

Scripture Reading: Matthew 21:8–9 — *Hosanna to the Son of David!*

Family Devotion Activity: Wave branches or draw palm leaves together. Shout "Hosanna!" as a family prayer.

Closing Blessing: May your home be filled with Hosanna joy, and your hearts open to the King.

WEEK 6: HOLY WEEK – THE TRIDUUM

Maundy Thursday: The Servant Meal

Daily Prayer: Jesus, thank You for showing us love through service. Help us serve one another with humility.

Reflection Prompt: What does it mean to love through service?

Scripture Reading: John 13:14–15 — *Now that I, your Lord and Teacher, have washed your feet...*

Family Devotion Activity: Share a simple meal together. Pray before eating, thanking God for love and service.

Closing Blessing: May your table be a place of love, and your hands ready to serve.

WEEK 6: HOLY WEEK — THE TRIDUUM

Good Friday: At the Cross

Daily Prayer: Lord, we remember Your sacrifice. Help us carry Your love in our hearts.

Reflection Prompt: What does the cross mean to you today?

Scripture Reading: John 19:30 — *It is finished.*

Family Devotion Activity: Light a candle and sit in quiet reflection. Share one word that comes to mind.

Closing Blessing: May the cross remind you of love beyond measure, and hope beyond sorrow.

WEEK 6: HOLY WEEK — THE TRIDUUM

Holy Saturday: Waiting in Hope

Daily Prayer: God, teach us to wait with trust, even when answers seem far away.

Reflection Prompt: What are you waiting for in hope?

Scripture Reading: Psalm 130:5 — *I wait for the Lord, my whole being waits...*

Family Devotion Activity: Write prayers of waiting and place them in a box or jar.

Closing Blessing: May waiting deepen your trust, and hope anchor your soul.

WEEK 6: HOLY WEEK – THE TRIDUUM

Easter Sunday: He Is Risen!

Daily Prayer: Risen Lord, thank You for the joy of resurrection. Fill us with Your life and light.

Reflection Prompt: Where do you see signs of resurrection in your life today?

Scripture Reading: Matthew 28:6 — *He is not here; He has risen!*

Family Devotion Activity: Step outside at sunrise. Sing or shout "Alleluia!" together.

Closing Blessing: May resurrection joy fill your home, and may hope rise with the dawn.

Family Journaling Prompt

How did we experience the journey of Holy Week—from Hosanna joy to resurrection hope?

Journal Notes:

_____
_____
_____
_____
_____
_____
_____
_____
_____
_____
_____
_____

WEEK 6: HOLY WEEK — THE TRIDUUM

_____
_____
_____
_____
_____
_____

Family Notes & Journaling

This section is provided for your own reflections, prayers, and family memories during Lent and Easter. Use these pages to write down thoughts, gratitude lists, or creative responses to the daily devotions.

Themed Prompt: Forgiveness

Reflect on a moment when you offered or received forgiveness. How did it bring peace?

_____
_____
_____
_____
_____
_____
_____
_____
_____

Themed Prompt: Renewal

Note one area of your life where you sense God inviting you to begin again.

_____
_____
_____
_____
_____
_____
_____
_____
_____
_____
_____

Themed Prompt: Family Connection

Record a memory of sharing faith together this week. What made it meaningful?

_____
_____
_____
_____
_____
_____
_____
_____
_____
_____

Themed Prompt: Joy

Capture a moment of joy you experienced during Lent. How did it remind you of God's love?

_____
_____
_____
_____
_____
_____
_____
_____
_____
_____
_____

Themed Prompt: Resurrection

Reflect on what Easter means to you personally. How does it change your perspective?

_____

_____

_____

_____

_____

_____

_____

_____

_____

_____

About the Author

Veronica Ruff is an Australian author and creative curator whose work blends faith, family, and sanctuary. She designs devotionals that nurture connection across generations through simple rhythms of prayer, reflection, and joy.

Her books integrate journaling prompts, colouring motifs, and family activities—creating gentle spaces where faith can be both personal and shared.

Veronica is passionate about publishing with integrity, ensuring clarity, harmony, and accessibility in every detail. She continues to develop seasonal projects that celebrate family rituals, including Easter and Christmas companion books.

She lives in New South Wales, where her home and garden form a sanctuary of creativity, care, and renewal.

Veronica is also the author of *When Work Becomes War*, available on Amazon.

https://amzn.asia/d/5dePXA2

www.ingramcontent.com/pod-product-compliance
Lightning Source LLC
Chambersburg PA
CBHW071322080526
44587CB00018B/3315